Patient 12

Kevin Summers

CURRENCY PRESS
The performing arts publisher

CURRENCY PLAYS

First published in 2014
by Currency Press Pty Ltd,
Gadigal Land, PO Box 2287, Strawberry Hills, NSW, 2012, Australia
enquiries@currency.com.au
www.currency.com.au
in association with La Mama Theatre, Melbourne.
Reprinted in 2023.
Copyright: © Kevin Summers, 2011, 2014.

COPYING FOR EDUCATIONAL PURPOSES
The Australian *Copyright Act 1968* (Act) allows a maximum of one chapter or 10% of this book, whichever is the greater, to be copied by any educational institution for its educational purposes provided that that educational institution (or the body that administers it) has given a remuneration notice to Copyright Agency (CA) under the Act.

For details of the CA licence for educational institutions contact CA, 12/66 Golbourn Street, Sydney, NSW, 2000. Tel: within Australia 1800 066 844 toll free; outside Australia +61 2 9394 7600; Fax: +61 2 9394 7601;
Email: memberservices@copyright.com.au

COPYING FOR OTHER PURPOSES
Except as permitted under the Act, for example a fair dealing for the purposes of study, research, criticism or review, no part of this book may be reproduced, stored in a retrieval system, or transmitted in any form or by any means without prior written permission. All enquiries should be made to the publisher at the address above.

Any performance or public reading of *Patient 12* is forbidden unless a licence has been received from the author or the author's agent. The purchase of this book in no way gives the purchaser the right to perform the play in public, whether by means of a staged production or a reading. All applications for public performance should be addressed to the author c/− Currency Press.

NATIONAL LIBRARY OF AUSTRALIA CIP DATA

Author:	Summers, Kevin, author.
Title:	Patient 12 / Kevin Summers.
ISBN:	9781925005103 (paperback)
Series:	Current theatre series.
Subject:	Military hospitals—Victoria—Melbourne—Drama.
	World War, 1914−1918—Participation, Australian—Drama.
	Australia—History—1901−1922—Drama.
Dewey Number:	A822.4

Typeset by Dean Nottle for Currency Press.
Cover design by Simon Russell, The Pound Project.
Cover photography by JEFF BUSBY.

Currency Press acknowledges the Traditional Owners of the Country on which we live and work. We pay our respects to all Aboriginal and Torres Strait Islander Elders, past and present.

Contents

Playwright's Note   v

PATIENT 12   1

Theatre Program at the end of the playtext

Here was the world's worst wound. And here with pride
'Their name liveth forever,' the Gateway claims.
Was ever an immolation so belied
As these intolerably nameless names?
Well might the Dead who struggled in the slime
Rise and deride this sepulchre of crime.

Siegfried Sassoon
'On Passing the new Menin Gate'

PLAYWRIGHT'S NOTE

It was a mere footnote. A scrap of reportage in a book about Australians in the Great War. The book was forgotten but the note remained in my memory: in a Sydney repatriation hospital a sad queue of people would file past to view an AIF soldier motionless and silent in his bed in the hope of identifying him as their son, brother, husband or lover.

The boy had been retrieved unconscious from the mud of Flanders and shipped home. But that simple and abject fact raised so many questions. How could he survive the injuries—presumably from continued shelling—and the long journey home sustained by nourishment only through primitive tubes? Why Sydney and not another city? Who had recorded him as coming from New South Wales? And what were the thoughts of these men and women who had received the dreaded cable informing them of the loss of their son and were now clinging to a vague hope that the boy may be theirs?

Such was the basis of *Patient 12*. A body in a bed. A jaded hospital doctor trying to do something decent. A small collection of folk taking a deep breath before stepping through a curtain to look at a body beyond ready identification. The hospital full of men with ruined bodies and disordered minds.

The play offers no more than a snapshot of postwar Australia, of a country injured and confused by the carnage of 1914–18. No family was immune from its effects. No town could escape the memories of loss and civil division. Time seemed incapable of healing; in many repat hospitals, in places similar to Caulfield, men would see out their years in both physical and mental agony. Bedridden men were still coughing out the bloodied contents of their lungs decades after their return.

In the light of a trend to a mindless celebration of 'blood sacrifice', of our nation being formed in battle, it can be argued that nothing good, not one damned thing, came out of World War One. This play is a pillar of that contention.

Kevin Summers
March 2014

Patient 12 had its first reading at La Mama Theatre, Melbourne, on 3 December 2011, with the following cast:

PATIENT 12	Daniel Niceski
DR CHARLES THOMAS	Chris Bunworth
VICTORIA DURHAM	Jenny Seedsman
ALEXANDER DURHAM	Colin MacPherson
PERCY GROVES	Tim Potter
EDWARD DENMANN	Ian Rooney
ALICE BATES	Ngaire Dawn Fair
NARRATOR	Peter Stratford

Patient 12 was first produced by La Mama Theatre, Melbourne, on 23 April 2014, with the following cast:

DR CHARLES THOMAS	Jason Buckley
ALEXANDER DURHAM	Colin MacPherson
VICTORIA DURHAM	Jenny Seedsman
PERCY GROVES	Joel Parnis
EDWARD DENMANN	Dennis Coard
ALICE BATES	Heidi Valkenberg
PATIENT 12 / JAMES DURHAM / ANDY DENMANN / FREDDIE DAMIANI / LEO	Will Ewing

Director, Don Mackay
Designer, Sophie Woodward
Lighting Designer, Bronwyn Pringle
Stage Manager, Chris Martin
Assistant Stage Manager, Libby Wilhelm

CHARACTERS

DR CHARLES THOMAS, Assistant Medical Officer, Caulfield Military Hospital, 50s
ALEXANDER DURHAM, Melbourne solicitor, 40s
VICTORIA DURHAM, his wife, 40s
PERCY GROVES, hospital patient, 20s
EDWARD DENMANN, miner, 50s
ALICE BATES, waitress, early 20s

PATIENT 12/ JAMES DURHAM / ANDY DENMANN / FREDDY DAMIANI / LEO (all played by the same actor)

SETTING

Early 1919. Caulfield Military Hospital: a small office area. The dominant feature is a bed veiled by a blue curtain. Thomas' crowded desk stage front. Files stacked on tables. A few scattered chairs. A case, or a number of boxes, containing letters.

Other scenes in flashback rendered by light changes.

Spotlights where characters read or recite letters from the case as required.

Clothing alters little during the course of the play. A different hat, tie or jacket will suffice.

STYLE AND DESIGN

The play has been constructed to be performed simply. It demands the one space only and relies on lighting to frame changes in time and place.

It is constructed as a meditation upon the intense divisions within our society in the year of 1919.

MUSIC

The cast sing the popular songs of the First World War era as a background to the action. They are in no sense intended to be musical numbers, just to set the period.

As it is a live performance, the live medium for the music is being used, rather than a recorded sound track.

Sometimes the music is used as a counterpoint to the action.

This play went to press before the end of rehearsals and may differ from the play as performed.

Will Longstaff's painting, Menin Gate at Midnight, *is reflected on a backdrop. Lights fade to black.*

Lights come up slowly on the hospital area. Not a dormitory but rather a corner of an office. Upstage is a bed veiled by a blue hospital curtain. We never see more than a glimpse of the bed in which a heavily bandaged figure lies. Slightly to the side is a large wooden desk with many papers surrounded by files. The space is cramped and in a state of flux. A stack of old cases which may contain old papers, photos and letters.

Music slowly up—'Keep the Home Fires Burning'. The rising glow of a lamp from behind the curtain.

DR THOMAS *emerges from the bed. He has been taking notes. The music fades.*

THOMAS: No face. No identification. No prospects of recovery.

He walks downstage and throws his notes on his cluttered desk.

And that silly bloody tattoo.

He sits and writes.

Some lettering, a 'D' certainly…

His writing is interrupted by a young man, PERCY GROVES. *He wears a plain white shirt (which sports the blue armband of hospital inmates) and dark trousers. He is holding a poorly made basket. His gait is a measured shuffle, his speech emerges in waves, followed by short silences. His mouth twitches.*

PERCY: Lovely day, lovely day. Outside. Sun is up, in my face. Feels good, very good indeed, doc.

THOMAS: Hello, Percy. Good to see you've been hard at work.

PERCY *is uncomprehending.* THOMAS *points to the basket.*

You've been weaving. That's good.

PERCY: Only started yesterday. No, the day before. Day before, that's right… Got help, though. Getting better.

THOMAS: Fine. Stick with it. Now, I have a lot of work to do.

PERCY*'s attention turns to the bed.*

Off you go now.

PERCY *shuffles toward the bed.* THOMAS *reacts.*
You hear me?

The young man continues, forcing THOMAS *to cut across him.*

I have told you before—you cannot go there. Leave him be. Understand?

PERCY: Need to see him… Need to talk. Catch up on old times.

THOMAS: You know the patient cannot talk.

PERCY: I want to talk. I want to talk. Leo can listen. I have lots to tell him… About everything. [*Extending the basket*] I made this for Leo.

THOMAS: Listen to me… yet again. Patient 12 fought at Menin Road during the advance of the 5th and 6th Battalions in October, 1917. We know that. We also know that you, Percy, were not at Menin Road at that time. I've been checking a lot of records lately.

PERCY: At Y… Ypres. In reserve. That's it.

THOMAS: Perhaps so. Then stop this nonsense by telling me Leo's full name.

PERCY: Can't… remember.

THOMAS: [*exasperated*] That's it then. Off you go, Percy. Go back to your group.

> THOMAS *escorts* PERCY *from the room. The younger man has little strength and offers no real resistance.*

PERCY: [*exiting*] Goodbye, Leo. I know you're there. Leo…

> THOMAS *struggles with the effort. Looks to* PATIENT 12. *Lights down.*

> *Spotlight on a prosperous-looking middle-aged couple—* ALEXANDER *and* VICTORIA DURHAM. *They speak their letters sent to their son James, stationed in England preparing to embark for northern France in 1917.*

> *The letters are taken from an old case, as featured in many homes, a place to store mementoes.*

DURHAM: My dear James, so pleased your arrival in Plymouth was uneventful. One reads much of the activities of Hun subs at the approaches to the English Channel that in this case I am delighted by your state of boredom. I know you will enjoy your time in London. It is a great city, the hub of the civilised world. Forget the weather. May I remind you, if you have the time, to visit old Mrs Hibbins at Swiss Cottage. She has heard so much about you over the years and I do feel I owe her so much for looking after me during my time at Gray's Inn.

VICTORIA: Hope the socks fit, dear. Had fallen out of the habit of knitting and would you believe how stiff and sore my fingers were? Margaret Beames from the Glenferrie Red Cross sends her best. You remember her boy, Keith? He is advancing somewhere in Palestine. Margaret says he is now on better terms with his camel which is finally starting to accept him and at times is quite sweet-natured. He would rather have a horse though and is taking a lot of ribbing from his old friends.

DURHAM: Butch is doing well. Of course he misses you very much and is looking forward to your return. He is eating like a wolf and demands his evening walks. He is a loyal dog.

VICTORIA: Mr Hughes' second referendum is going to be a close vote, it appears. Not for one minute can I understand this. The 'no' argument is again led by that vile Roman Catholic cleric Mannix, who is only interested in hurting Britain to promote the cause of Ireland. Yet so much has already been done with the *Home Rule Act*. Why are they so vindictive? Why do they support the Germans? I cannot bear to think of the consequences if conscription is rejected again.

DURHAM: The local Court of Petty Sessions still provides me with plenty of employment, though of the depressing kind. Liquor is a curse and the basis of much crime, as much among women as men. This lack of moral fibre flies in the face of this young nation's deeds at Gallipoli and now in Europe. I fear there is a great divide between exemplary defence of Empire and the base opportunism that surrounds me.

VICTORIA: Despite all the home troubles, we read in all the papers that the war is going well and the Kaiser may soon abdicate and Germany will sue for peace. I pray for this—and for you—all my waking hours.

DURHAM: Look forward to hearing from you soon. One other matter— you must get to the Queen's House at Greenwich. A most beautiful structure—Inigo Jones' little masterpiece. You'll like it very much.

VICTORIA: Keep safe, dear James. Your loving mother… Victoria.

DURHAM: Bring those Huns to heel. The only good German is a dead one. Your proud father… Alexander.

Lights down.

THOMAS *at his desk. Agitated, he rises and paces as he reads from his notes.*

THOMAS: At 4.40 this morning the night nurse observed that his eyes opened for some seconds without blinking. 12 remains a patient of interest and I shall continue to monitor his patterns. Feeding program via tubes is surprisingly efficient, with few signs of infection. Chance of recovery—nil

He moves to the curtain, parts it and peers at the figure.

Who the hell are you? And what to do with you? Well, my silent friend, you've done your bit for King and country, so I'll do what I can for you. I'll try not to let you die alone.

He walks to his desk but stops.

You didn't hear that, did you?

He laughs weakly.

Lights down.

Spotlight on a rough-hewn middle-aged man—EDWARD DENMANN. *He wears the rugged, functional clothes of the working class. He speaks his letter.*

DENMANN: Andy. You know I'm not too good at writing and I said I would not but here I am, doing same. And I know I said I would not do so under any conditions but that was the grog talking. It's pretty crook down here at Korumburra. Things have got much worse. The mine bosses are trying to put all of us off wages and onto piecework. They are mongrels. The police have come down from Melbourne to watch the place. Think they would have better things to do than do the bosses' dirty work…

Well, Andy, look after yourself. You made your decision. Stay in one piece. Your dad.

One more bit—you may not feel like writing but if you do then that would be good with me.

Lights down.

PERCY *enters the room carrying a kerosene lamp. He finds a chair and sits.*

PERCY: Doc Thomas is smart, Leo. Wants… wants me to tell him about you. Who you, who you are. No good there. Then I'll lose you. Lose you. He gets mad and says I can't see you... Says I'll be kicked out if I'm found with you. Can't have that. Nowhere to go. Not now... Tried back at the farm. No good, Leo, no good at all. Didn't want me up there. Too much trouble. Said I was a... d... disruption. Said that. My mother... said that to me. Made me cry. She cried too. We all cried. Too many tears. Started a flood. Noah's Ark needed.

The lamp renders his face a ghostly mask.

Dr Thomas is a good man. I think he is a good man... Grumpy, though. Oh, grumpy. Always got his goat up. Very busy. On the go with so many here. You'll like it here, Leo... Lots of people coming and going. And we make lots of things here. I made a lovely basket for you the other day but it was taken from me to sell and I'll have to make you another one. A better one.

And we sing, Leo. Sing a lot. You'll like that. You and your lovely voice. All the best songs, not just religious...

[*Sung, with difficulty, almost whispering*]
As I walk along the Boo Boolong...
With an independent air,
You can hear the girls declare
He must be a millionaire...

Hey, Leo. Not so loud. They'll hear you.

[*Sung*] You can hear them sigh and... wish to die
You can see them wink the other eye
At the man who broke the bank at Monte Carlo.

Sshh. Oh, Leo, you are a card. But seriously, there'll be trouble... They'll get rid of me. Cart me off somewhere else again. No room, they'll say. I won't see you. Be quiet. Please.

He looks about, rises and splits the curtain.

It's good to... see you again, Leo.

The lamp is extinguished.

Spotlight on an attractive young woman. She is wearing cheap but stylish attire. Her name is ALICE BATES *and she also recites a letter from the case. Her upbeat words are slightly at odds with her reserved delivery.*

ALICE: 24th October, 1916. Darling Freddy. Got your letter from Boulogne, if that's how it's spelt. It all sounds grand. Keep away from those French girls. I've heard they are loose. So don't give them the eye, alright. At least the weather over there seems to be picking up. Too cold for me over there. Sorry you got docked your pay. Try to obey some orders. Can't be that hard to salute!

I worked at the Caulfield Cup the other day. The extra pounds will come in handy. You wouldn't know a war was on with the size of the crowd. And thirsty too. I worked like a navvy all day and then had to get to Young and Jackson's to serve the same blokes for the last hour. This six o'clock closing is stupid. They climb over each other at the bar to get served before the clock strikes. Mad buggers. They drink so quick that some bring it up straight away. The mess! We're the ones left to clean up. No-one likes it, except the Women's Temperance Union.

You probably have already heard by the time you get this letter that Shepherd King won the Cup. Would have liked to see the race but too frantic. Funny that he's an English horse who was shipped to Melbourne when you boys were heading to Egypt, like there was no war at all. Perhaps you waved to him as you crossed at sea. Or he waived to you!

The referendum is next Saturday and it's going to be close. I looked at all the men at the races and there's lots and lots not in khaki. Able-looking types to me. Of course the members was full of them in their best clothes. The types who tell others to go off to fight. Could not help but feel a bit poor about it, with you over there. I hope the censors let this go through.

Well, that's about all for now. The house saw out the winter fine, though things are getting dearer in Footscray, and my wedding dress is ready for the time you come back safe and sound. Keep writing when you have the time. And keep your head down.

Yours ever, with love and tickles.
Alice.

Lights down.

Lights up. THOMAS *leans on his desk. He stares towards the bed. After some time* DURHAM *and* VICTORIA *emerge from behind the curtain. They have had private time with* PATIENT 12. THOMAS *rises to meet them.*

THOMAS: You can take more time if...

DURHAM: No, no thank you, doctor. It was quite sufficient.

THOMAS: Never going to be easy. I'm sorry but there are some questions...

VICTORIA: We understand.

THOMAS *arranges some chairs for them.*

THOMAS: I need to stress to you, Mr and Mrs Durham, that there is perhaps only a slight chance that Patient 12 is your son. I know that sounds a little severe and I, eh, don't wish to dishearten you, but it would be dishonest of me to build your hopes.

DURHAM: Dr Thomas, you have no idea how much your letter meant to us. May I remind you the previous official letter we received was to inform us that our only son was missing, believed killed.

THOMAS: Of course, of course. Now, your son—

VICTORIA: James.

THOMAS: Yes, James... Medium height, build.

DURHAM: Correct.

THOMAS: His teeth? No dentures?

VICTORIA: Regular. All his own.

THOMAS: Good.

DURHAM: But with all the wrapping, the bandages... Do we know?

THOMAS: They are often removed to allow the skin to breathe. Then to apply moisture, antiseptic, to the skin. [*Pause.*] The lad has no lips. The mouth is fully exposed. He has no face at all. I thought I made it plain in my letter to you.

DURHAM: Yes, you did, doctor. I must have... put it to the side of my mind.

THOMAS: Yes. Now, I need to turn to his tattoo. As you saw, the scar tissue over that area makes clarification difficult but I have enlisted the help of local tattoo proprietors and police experts. It could be— among others—the name Durham. Did your boy—?

VICTORIA: James. His name is James.

THOMAS: Did James ever tell you, either before he embarked or later, that he had acquired a tattoo?

DURHAM: No, he didn't. But I hear that it was very common among troops to get one. Here, or Egypt or London. I'm sure Paris was full of such… establishments, and he was there for a while. That's right, yes?

THOMAS: Wouldn't he have written to you about getting it?

DURHAM: Perhaps he wanted to surprise us… when he came home. Perhaps he had weightier matters on his mind at the time.

THOMAS: Of course.

VICTORIA: I held his hand. I held his hand in mine.

THOMAS: [*to* DURHAM] So physically he could be your son?

VICTORIA: That was his hand I held. That is James. Also the contour of his face. I'm quite sure.

THOMAS: Mrs Durham, his hands have been shattered and burnt. As I said, his face is a—

VICTORIA: I know my son.

DURHAM: Victoria, let's not rush to judgement. Please.

VICTORIA: I'm not one of your legal clients.

An uncomfortable quiet.

THOMAS: Please, Mr and Mrs Durham. It was with the greatest reluctance that I wrote to all possible kin of this soldier. A year ago you received the letter that broke your hearts. Now I've sent you a letter telling you your son may be alive. But please, understand this—it's a false dawn. Patient number 12 is so named because since the Armistice eleven other lads have been repatriated here with little or no hope of recovery. At least they can share a dormitory and they respond in some way—a nod or a smile perhaps. And they have a name, an identity. The very presence of this silent soldier upsets the other patients. Do you follow?

He rises and partially opens the curtain. The figure on the bed is partly visible.

This man has no face. His body is broken into pieces. His skin is a rancid, weeping membrane. Fluids ooze in and then out. Thus far he has escaped infection. The best part of the story is that he is brain dead—at least I pray to God that he is—and that he will die sooner rather than later. Are you listening to this, Mrs Durham?

Silence. THOMAS *sits.*

I'm sorry. Very sorry.

VICTORIA: You pray to God, doctor. You're a religious man then?

THOMAS: No, I... used it more as a figure of speech—to make my point. I have no real belief in God, Mrs Durham. If you must know I lost whatever faith I had in the South African War, at a place called Middleburg, in the Transvaal. Quite a pretty place, if you like such places for a spot of bloodletting.

VICTORIA: I'm sorry your faith was so brittle. I believe in God, sir, and I believe this man will live and recover if it is God's will.

THOMAS: Then by all means pray for his welfare but my medical opinion is this—beyond his other injuries his brain has suffered massive concussion. While lying for days out there in no-man's-land he was thrown about like a rag doll. Imagine that his skull had been kicked by heavy boots over a twenty-minute period. That's about as reasonable an example I can think of.

DURHAM: But you said he opens his eyes.

THOMAS: An involuntary reflex, nothing more. I have concluded that he is brain dead.

DURHAM: But you can't be a hundred percent certain, can you, doctor?

THOMAS: [*after a pause*] No. As a lawyer you know that very little is black and white. If you want to play with percentages, I'll say that I'm ninety-five percent certain that Patient 12 has no active brain life.

A house bell rings.

I'm needed elsewhere. A nurse will be attending to his tubes and bandages in a few minutes. You are welcome to stay till then. I expect we shall be seeing more of each other in the coming weeks. Good day.

He exits. DURHAM *appears crestfallen. His wife is more positive.*

DURHAM: [*making to leave*] Let's go home. Victoria?

VICTORIA: What do you mean? Go home? We have found our son— and you want to go home?

DURHAM: You heard Dr Thomas.

VICTORIA: And you believe him? I don't, not for a minute. We need to talk to James, to let him know we are at his side, that we love him.

DURHAM: We don't know for certain it's him. It may be someone else.

VICTORIA: Don't talk like that. I don't want to hear that sort of rubbish.

PERCY *enters. He does not immediately notice the couple, intent on moving toward the curtain.*

PERCY: Just saw Thomas doing his rounds, Leo. In the dormitories.

He sees the pair and starts. Silence.

DURHAM: Hello.

PERCY *nods.*

What's your name?

PERCY: Percy Groves… Why? Am I in trouble?

DURHAM: I don't think so.

VICTORIA: Who's Leo?

PERCY: Don't know… what you mean. No idea.

VICTORIA: When you came in you looked over to the man in the bed and called him Leo.

PERCY: Did I?… No, I didn't. Not me. Someone else.

VICTORIA: [*impatient*] You called him Leo. I want to know why.

DURHAM: Victoria, enough.

PERCY *makes to speak but looks to the bed, confused. He runs off.*

The lad is mentally damaged. He doesn't know what he's saying, for heaven's sake. We really should be getting home.

VICTORIA: We can stay here with James until the nurse comes—and that's what we shall do.

She turns upstage, parts the curtain and goes to the bed. DURHAM *watches her but does not move.*

Lights down.

Soundscape of a public meeting. Cheers and jeers, catcalls and whistling.

Lights up on the figure of EDWARD DENMANN *at a simple lectern. The Australian flag is draped on it. He is combative, hectoring his audience.*

DENMANN: Prime Minister Hughes calls men like me foul parasites attacking the vitals of labour. Well, Hughes would know all about hitting below the belt. He has profited from his betrayal of the Australian working class by climbing into bed with the financiers and the war mongers.

He calls us traitors when in fact he's the traitor. Years ago Hughes was a true man of the working class. No longer. He says the Industrial Workers of the World know no nationality. The little rat is dead right about that. We hold that all men and women are equal under the sun, don't matter if they're British, German, Turkman, Japanese or Australian. What's important is to be true to your class, not your country.

INTERJECTOR: You're a low dog.

Cheers and jeers, rising in intensity.

DENMANN: Call me what you like, but you can't beat an idea when it's ready to spread about the world. Hughes says we have no religion—well, he's wrong again. We worship at the shrine of true labour in its struggle with capital. For who are the real victors of this filthy rotten war? The bankers and the bond holders—both British and German. The very men who demand that mothers give up their sons to fight other mothers' sons, men who have no grievance with each other. And now Hughes and his fat capitalist mates are demanding that our boys are conscripted to die in a ditch for them, to die so that the armaments kings, the Krupps of Germany and the Vickers of England, can continue to make their millions. Or that the squattocracy here can raise the price of wool and wheat in scarce times to make their pile.

The war is, has been and forever will be a sham. The press barons of both sides tell us that the enemy is barbaric. They create a feeling of hatred when in fact there is no natural hatred between workers. None. In fact, they are brothers, comrades. Yet the robber barons of industry and of the press command that they must battle each other in the mud of France. For what? So that their dirty, stinking empires might flourish and continue to force half the world into slavery.

INTERJECTOR: We've heard enough of you, you traitor. You're not a true Australian!

DENMANN: I'll tell you what I am—a true internationalist. Flags like this mean nothing to me. It's a symbol of bloody oppression.

He grabs the ensign, rolls it up and throws it to the ground. Sounds of a possible riot. DENMANN *prepares to defend himself amid the rising crowd noise.*

Come on, you piss weak bastards! Come on!

Lights down as the sounds of general mayhem cease.

Lights up on PERCY, *quietly slipping into the area in front of the curtain. He sits and recites, trying hard to remember the verse.*

PERCY: The world has got snouted jist a treat
Crool Forchin's dirty left 'as smote me soul…
An' all them joys o' life… I 'eld so sweet is up the pole.
Fer, as the poit sez, me 'eart 'as got the pip wiv yearnin' fer—I dunno what.

The curtain parts and LEO *enters. He is dressed as a private of the AIF. He walks to* PERCY, *carrying military-issue rain covers. He takes up the verse.*

LEO: I'm crook; me name is mud; I've done me dash;
Me flamin' spirit's got the flamin' 'ump;
I'm longin' to let loose on somethin' rash—Aw, I'm a chump.
I know it; but his blimed ole Springtime craze
Fair outs me on these dilly, silly days.

He gently places the cover on PERCY *and sits next to him, also covering himself.*

Geez, Percy, you'll catch your death, dressed like that. It's an English summer, you know. Least this will keep the wind out.

PERCY: [*now speaking without difficulty*] They breed us tough in the Kiewa Valley, not like you lot from the cities.

LEO: You're the only idiot I know who reckons Shepparton is a city. And the only dill who can't learn more than one verse of 'The Sentimental Bloke'.

PERCY: There's more to life than learning poetry or singing ditties to impress the girls.

LEO: As good a way as any. What's the secret of your undoubted success?

PERCY: Shut up.

Silence. LEO *again ensures that* PERCY *is protected from the cold wind. A simple but intimate act of friendship.*

LEO: So this is the beautiful English countryside?

PERCY: That's what they say.

LEO: It's not all it's cracked up to be. Pretty bloody ordinary. What's this place called?
PERCY: Hampstead.
LEO: You know the trouble, Perce? It's the noise.
PERCY: I can't hear much.
LEO: That's what I mean. It's so quiet, too quiet. Where are the birds? What I wouldn't do to hear a magpie—a proper magpie, not the little flappers they've got over here—or even a bloody galah. Just doesn't seem right.
PERCY: There'll be enough noise in France when we get there. Let's enjoy the peace and quiet.

Silence.

Are you nervous?
LEO: Nervous? Gee, nervous is opening the batting against Nagambie. This is different. Dunno what it is. A sort of gnawing in your guts, at least to me. I know I'll be up to it. I'll do my duty. But it's not the same feeling I had last year.
PERCY: Nah. We were all keen as mustard at Broadmeadows. The whole thing was a lark. The big adventure. The only thing we were frightened of then was missing out on the action.
LEO: Bit different when the boys are dying like flies and there's no end in sight. Could go on for years, they say. Puts the wind up ya.
PERCY: Still, better than pickin' fruit when it's on offer. Breakin' your back in the heat. Reckon our training will kick in and we'll do the right thing over there. I won't lie doggo or anything like that but… geez, Leo, I don't know if I can kill a man. That gets to me. I think all the time about that. Like this bloke, this Hun, is coming at me through the smoke, and I've my rifle at the ready and I can't get my finger to the trigger. It won't move. And Fritz is racing at me and his teeth are bared like a mad dog and I know he's going to get me but I don't do anything.
LEO: I think if he's about to do you in, mate, you'll react alright. Reckon you'll take him before he takes you. Stands to reason.
PERCY: Suppose so. But I won't be going out of my way to kill anybody in this war. Nothing will make me feel good about that.

Pause. They regard each other with quiet affection.

Sing to me, Leo.

LEO: Come on, Perce, you don't want to hear my droning.

PERCY: You know the one.

LEO: [*looking about*] Alright, but just a bit. I get embarrassed.

He stands and sings.

[*Sung*] As I walk along the Bois Boolong
With an independent air,
You can hear the girls declare
He must be a millionaire.

PERCY *stands and joins him.*

LEO & PERCY: [*sung*] You can see them sigh and wish to die
You can see them wink the other eye
At the man who broke the bank at Monte Carlo.

Quietly, LEO *takes the cover from* PERCY, *who continues to sing lustily, and exits behind the curtain.*

Light change.

PERCY: [*sung*] At the man who broke the bank at Monte Carlo.

A harried THOMAS *enters.*

THOMAS: What the hell are you doing, Groves? Get out of here. Did you see Patient 12 against my orders?

PERCY *does not immediately respond. When he does his speech reverts to the prior pattern.*

PERCY: No, sir, doctor. Just standing here… singing, sir, singing. You told me not to go there.

THOMAS: [*softening*] Glad you're in a good frame of mind, Percy, but it's all too much. What if everyone went about singing all the time? Too horrible to contemplate, all that fun. You know we have specific times for communal singing. You follow?

DENMANN *enters. He looks about, clearly discomforted and a little hung-over.* THOMAS *reacts.*

Off you go, Percy. Good man. It's nice outside. Take a walk in the gardens. Do you good.

PERCY *looks at* DENMANN, *obeys and exits.*

Edward Denmann?

DENMANN: I informed the hospital I'd be here today.

THOMAS: Charles Thomas, Deputy Medical Examiner. I wrote to you. Good of you to come.

DENMANN: Took me most of the day to get here from Korumburra and I'll have to find lodgings tonight... unless I can doss here.

THOMAS: Sorry, we cannot cope as it is. We're placing beds wherever we can. And what with the influenza... You should find something around the corner, in Glenhuntly Road. [*Pointing to the curtain*] This is Patient 12.

DENMANN: Right.

THOMAS: [*producing a sheet of paper*] This is the list of physical characteristics as I can best discern. I have plainly outlined the extreme difficulties...

DENMANN: Yeah. I read 'em.

THOMAS: And you took the trouble to get here.

DENMANN: Couldn't not come.

THOMAS: Look, Mr Denmann, his chances of survival—

DENMANN: Yeah, yeah, you wrote that too. I understand. Can I have a look?

THOMAS: Of course. Don't be shocked if he opens his eyes. It's not a sign of recovery. Take as long as you like.

DENMANN is taken aback but merely nods. He slowly walks to the curtain and goes through. THOMAS *exits.*

Light change.

DENMANN *emerges from behind the curtain. He is drunkenly angry.*

DENMANN: You bloody fool, Andy. I taught ya better than this.

His son, ANDY, *walks behind him, an AIF private.*

ANDY: Just settle down and listen for once.

DENMANN: You're throwing away your life. For what? For nothin'.

ANDY: I've enlisted to fight. I've done what every other bloke has done. Is that so wrong?

DENMANN: Yes, it is. Because you're not every other bloke. You know better. I've told you better.

ANDY: That's right, that's right. I forgot. You know everything—the tough-as-nails miner from the shit heaps of Gippsland.

DENMANN: The bloke who gave you tucker and a bunk and protection. You ungrateful... I oughta...

DENMANN *makes toward his son, who stands his ground.*

ANDY: You oughta what? Hit me? Is that the way out again? Well, come on—I'm right here. Have a go. But I'll tell you this, Dad—I'll let you knock me down but I'll get back up and sit you on your pants. It's taken twenty years but I reckon I can do it. Just give me the chance!

Father and son, suspended between their past and future. The older man gives way.

DENMANN: You're a strappin' young man, Andy. Too good for me.

ANDY: Well, that's something. 'Bout bloody time.

Pause.

DENMANN: Don't do this, Andy.

ANDY: I've held out as long as I could.

DENMANN: It's a mug's war.

ANDY: You think I don't know? That I've been deaf to you for all these years? You shout at life, Dad. How could I not hear you?

DENMANN: Then don't fight.

ANDY: Truth is, I'm not as strong as the great Ed Denmann. I guess I haven't got the balls. Did I tell you about the last time I got a white feather in the face? Not the first time, the last! That would have been a month ago in Warragul when a beautiful girl smiled at me as I left the post office there. I was just getting on my bike when she stuck the thing in my face. And a dozen people yelled at me—'Shirker, coward'. And I knew most of them, dad—I knew them.

DENMANN: They're nothin'. They're useless articles.

ANDY: 'Why aren't you doing the manly thing?' the girls yell at me. 'A traitor to the nation.' That's what I get all the time. I can't take it.

DENMANN: So you'd rather die for the bosses than take a razz from a few sheilas?

ANDY: I just want to be like everybody else. I don't want to fight your wars. I reckon I have to choose my own, or everybody else's. I'm not the strong, tough man you are; not the brawling, hard-drinking miner's hero, Big Ed.

DENMANN: I've dedicated me life to fighting for the workin' man. Nothin' more, nothin' less. And I'm sorry that you've taken no notice of me over the twenty years when I raised ya as best I could. I'm sorry you've done what you've done. So you go with your other stupid mates to France and fight other stupid blokes for no reason. You do that, Andy. But don't expect any letters from me tellin' you about how miserable the whole bloody situation is. Do what you bloody want but you won't be hearin' from me.

ANDY: Then you can go to buggery.

ANDY paces off toward the curtain. DENMANN watches him go for some time.

Light change.

ALICE enters, looking lost.

ALICE: Are you the doctor?

DENMANN: Do I look like a doctor?

ALICE: Sorry. I'm looking for Freddy, Freddy Damiani.

DENMANN: Eyetie?

ALICE: That a problem?

DENMANN: [*laughing*] Na, love, not at all.

ALICE: They wrote and told me he was in here somewhere. Number 12. They said he was Patient 12.

DENMANN: [*pointing*] He's up there. They wrote to me too. You see, my name's Denmann. They're after people with names startin' with 'D' because of that tattoo on his chest. They tell you that?

ALICE: Yes. They write to many?

DENMANN: Dunno. You his missus?

ALICE: Fiancée. He had no other family. And you?

DENMANN: I'm his dad.

They share a slight smile at their situation.

ALICE: Freddy never had a tattoo.

DENMANN: Seems a lot of the troops got 'em in England, before they went off to fight. Though why Andy would want to put anything to do with me on his chest is anyone's guess.

ALICE: Yeah?

DENMANN: I wouldn't let him go. I despise the whole bloody war. I'm what they call a Wobbly.

ALICE: What's that?

DENMANN: Industrial Workers of the World. Like a giant union for all working folk. So I'm what they call a Wobbly.

ALICE: Funny name.

DENMANN: [*taking a deep breath*] They reckon it was because some Chinese members couldn't say it properly—came out like 'wobbly'.

ALICE: You're havin' me on.

DENMANN: Sounds like a load of… That's what I'm told. Whatever. The story is that I spend half me time locked up for opposing the war then one day me lad turns up in uniform. Took the wind fair out of me sails. [*Pause.*] But here I am. I had to come. Just like you, love. I'll leave him to ya.

ALICE: Alright then.

DENMANN: And don't get a shock if his eyes pop open. Don't mean a thing, the doc says. His brain has turned to mush.

DENMANN *exits.*

Light change. Spotlight on ALICE. *Again, she recites a letter from the case.*

ALICE: Dear Freddy. Got you letter from Abbeville. Seems you've had a pretty rough time of it. Keep yourself well. Keep your head down. The war drags on and on. Every day the papers are full of good news from the front yet it goes on. There's lots of mutterings now about when it's going to be all over. Now there are men on the street going about without arms and legs and bad eyes. Awful to see.

Freddy—I don't want you to send any more money to me. That would be dishonest of me because of what I have to tell you. I have been keeping company with a man. He is a police constable who has been working out of the Russell Street Barracks. He patrols around Young and Jackson's. That's where I met him.

I'm not sure if I'm in love with this man but I now know I don't love you like you might want me to. This is awfully hard to write but I have to tell you my true feelings. I know we've only had each other in this world for the past three years but I think I was too young to make good decisions. Please don't be upset. You know that you were the first man I have known—that will always be so.

I will keep all your belongings carefully in the house and hope to see you as soon as you get back. Please don't be upset about this. It's for the best.

Affectionately yours.

Alice.

ALICE *thinks about leaving as she returns the letter but steels herself and parts the curtain.*

Lights down.

Lights up on PERCY *who sits in contemplation for some time.* LEO *runs out, playing with a cricket ball.*

LEO: Percy!

He throws the ball overarm to his friend.

Catch!

PERCY *catches cleanly.*

Good one. Mind you, no place for dropped catches in the trenches. Catch a German grenade clean as a whistle and lob it back, eh, Perce?

PERCY: I never had much of a throwing arm.

LEO *takes the ball and demonstrates his style again.*

LEO: It's easy. [*Indicating the ball*] This is a standard mighty Mills' Bomb. Turn your shoulder away from the target. Keep the arm straight—that gives you accuracy—and turn.

He tosses to PERCY *who again catches neatly.*

Have a go.

PERCY *rises and produces a decent throw but quickly loses interest.*

PERCY: That alright?

LEO: Yeah. Good enough for Fritz. [*Pause.*] Hey, you're the best rifleman in the whole dam battalion. You don't need to throw grenades…

He sits at PERCY*'s side.*

Bomb-thrower, sniper—in the end we're the bloody infantry. And to be an infantryman you need a strong back and a weak head. That right?

LEO's *levity has little impact on* PERCY.

PERCY: We're going to be separated.

LEO: Who knows?… Probably. Stands to reason. Different skills and all. We won't be far apart, though. You can bet your last shilling on that.

PERCY: Yeah.

LEO: Percy, promise me this—if we do get away from each other, then don't lose your grip. Don't think too deep on anything. You heard what the old hands have had to say. Don't worry over the dead. For them, it's too late. They're gone. Think about you being alive and coming back at the end of every action. And I'll do the same and we'll find each other and we'll laugh and laugh. Promise me that, Perce.

PERCY: I said a while back that I didn't want to kill out there… I'm not too keen on dying out there either.

LEO *places his arm on* PERCY's *shoulder.*

LEO: No, mate, none of us wants to die out there. Greedy buggers, aren't we?

Lights out.

Music—'Hail, Hail, the Gang's All Here'. Trails off during THOMAS's *words.*

Lights up on THOMAS *at the desk, writing. Obviously tired, a little distressed. He's also had a drink or two.*

THOMAS: 12/10/1919. Influenza, the so-called Spanish Flu, is now firmly established in Victoria, despite our best efforts. The virus is like nothing I have ever dealt with, attacking the young and strong rather than the old and infirm. As such, it presents a lethal threat to both recovering patients and all staff members. A healthy man can sicken and die in the space of days. And we have no way of stopping it.

More victims of what is now referred to as 'shell shock' continue to be admitted. They are in a terrible state and no-one knows what to do with them. Government action lags in this area. Repeat, government action lags.

Patient 12 remains somewhere between life and death. He is taking up valuable space and resources, yet we are no closer to resolving the matter of his identity. I fear I have created a rod for my back and as for those…

As he writes, ALICE *enters. He rises.*

Miss Bates.

ALICE: I've come to tell you that I won't be coming in again.

THOMAS: I can hardly blame you for that. It must be very difficult.

ALICE: I don't think it's him. It's not Freddy.

THOMAS: You knew him. It's fine. [*Pause.*] Why did you come? You didn't need to… A letter would do.

ALICE: [*hesitantly*] I know… Can't really explain. Thought it was the decent thing.

THOMAS: When you leave, go to the side gate. You will avoid the flu patients.

ALICE: Ta. I've survived so far.

THOMAS: Then you have been very lucky, Miss Bates. Put this on.

He gives her a face mask and starts to exit. As he does, PERCY *enters.* THOMAS *deftly deals with him, escorting him off.* ALICE *puts on the mask and parts the curtain.*

Light change.

ALICE *runs out (no mask), chased by* FREDDY. *He is determinedly amorous. He grabs at her.*

ALICE: No, Freddy, not here. We got people everywhere.

FREDDY: Fuck 'em. Or better still, fuck you.

ALICE: Don't. Don't talk like that.

FREDDY: Like what? I'm only being affectionate. Come on, Al, I've got three days left. Show me you love me.

He drags her to the ground, all hands.

ALICE: I'll show you when we're at home. Not out here, you dill.

FREDDY: Bet those English girls'll come running. Not to mention the Froggie sheilas. Just dyin' to have a piece of Australia.

ALICE: Freddy!

FREDDY: You jealous?

ALICE: Be nice to me, Freddy.

He crudely kisses her.

FREDDY: Anythink ya want, dearie.

ALICE: God, Freddy, you look strange. You alright?

FREDDY: Freddy Damiani of Alfred Street, Footscray, Victoria, Australia, is mad as a cut snake. He's off to France to kill the Hun. And getting' paid to do it. Fancy me, a six-bob-a-day tourist in Frogland. Better than the shit I get now breakin' me back on the roads. I'll come home loaded—king of the two-up schools—and a fuckin' corporal with a load of medals.

ALICE: Just come home, never mind the rank and the medals.

FREDDY: And you'll be there, in Alfred Street?

ALICE: I'll be there. What do you reckon?

FREDDY: Cos I'm comin' back and everyone's gunna know about me. Let's go home and make a baby.

ALICE: You go home and make a baby. I've got to pick up stuff at the milk bar.

FREDDY: When I come back from France I want you ready to pop out a little Freddy.

ALICE: Please. It's not the right time. We've gone through this. When you get back…

FREDDY: And we've gone through this too, haven't we? I'll be back in a year and I want to be a dad. No fuckin' Hun is gunna lay me low. No ifs, no nuthin'. I'll be back in short order and I'll be knockin' on our door, Al.

Again he manhandles her.

Forget the milk bar.

ALICE: [*rising*] I'll see you at home.

FREDDY: Bugger off, then. I got mates at the Stanley Arms waitin' for me.

He starts to exit to the curtain.

ALICE: Don't, Freddy. Please. You'll only get drunk and…

He takes no notice and is gone through the curtain.

Light change. She moves slightly towards the curtain. Stops.

I don't want it to be you but if it is, I want you to die. [*Pause.*] Sorry, Freddy. You were handsome and strong and I felt things for you, I really did, but I lied when I wrote all those letters. Like I was convincing myself that I loved you, that you were everything. It was tough because we only had each other, but knowing other people—other men—made me see it all different. I thought you were good for me but you weren't, Freddy, you weren't. I now reckon you used me like I was a bit of... dunno...

... but nothing much, nothing special. I might be silly Alice behind the bar but I wanted to be treated fair.

You wanted a baby—I didn't. But you never asked me, not properly. I'm not ready. Not yet. Not in this sort of world with broken men and bad dreams and now germs we can't do anything about. I'm frightened.

When that letter came, the one that said you were likely dead, I didn't know how to feel. I half expected it, with that crazy way of yours, all guts and glory—be just like you to get a tatt but it wouldn't be my name. Then I thought of the thrashing and abuse I was likely to get when you got back knowing I wasn't yours anymore. Then I was glad, Freddy. So it is true that I want you to die—if that is you in there. They say you're a vegetable and that you'll die soon enough. That's to the good.

She exits.

Lights down. Music softly—'Mademoiselle from Armentières', gradually rising. From offstage we hear some raucous singing of the tune.

Lights up. It is PERCY *who enters singing. He seems drunk but it's hard to tell. He is trying to dance to the song, holding an imaginary French lass. He is unable to sing or dance to any effect.*

PERCY: [*sung*] ... hinkey dinkey parlez-vous?
    Oh, mademoiselle from Armentières, parlez-vous?
    Oh, mademoiselle from Armentières, parlez-vous?
    She's the hardest working girl in the town,
    But makes her living upside down,
    Hinkey dinkey parlez-vous?

The song stops abruptly as he spies the DURHAMS, *who have entered the space. Rather than retreat,* PERCY *grabs* VICTORIA *and dances her about the stage. His exuberance carries him along and she is little more than a rag doll in his arms.*

    [*Sung*] Oh, mademoiselle from Armentières, parlez-vous?
    Oh, mademoiselle from Armentières, parlez-vous?

VICTORIA: Alexander, get him off me!
PERCY: [*sung*] She'll do it for wine, she'll do it for rum,
   Sometimes for chocolate and chewing gum!

   DURHAM *takes control of* PERCY *and rescues his wife.*

DURHAM: Come on, old boy, there we go. Settle up.
PERCY: I met her. Not there, though. In Albert, and Abbeville... and Lille. All the places, all the *mademoiselles*.

   DURHAM *deftly calms* PERCY.

DURHAM: I'm sure you did. You must have been very popular, a fine young man like you.
PERCY: Best man in Tawonga... best... in Dederang.
VICTORIA: This is the boy who calls James 'Leo'.
DURHAM: Oh, yes. What was your name? You're in a happy mood today.
PERCY: Percy... Percy Groves. Best man in the Kiewa Valley. On the fire water today... Get it from me mates. [*Whispering*] Elsternwick Hotel. Not supposed to. Rules... Can't do it. Against rules. Never used to... to drink. Never. Do now. Like it, you see. You here to see Leo?
VICTORIA: [*to* DURHAM, *quietly*] He's drunk. Tell him to go away.
DURHAM: He's a patient here, Victoria. I don't think I can tell him to do that.
VICTORIA: I don't care. He gets on my nerves.
PERCY: Leo's doing well. Very well. He's talking...
VICTORIA: What?
PERCY: Just like old times. We sing too, sing and laugh.
VICTORIA: [*to her husband*] Could that be true? James is conscious?

   She turns her attention to the curtain.

DURHAM: [*whispering*] This boy doesn't know what he is saying. Look at him.

   An irate THOMAS *enters.*

THOMAS: Percy, I heard your noise from the other—
VICTORIA: Dr Thomas, is the patient awake?
THOMAS: No. As I have said to you, as I have written to you, the lad is not recovering. He will never recover.
PERCY: No, he talks to me. And we sing.
THOMAS: Be quiet, Percy. Have you been drinking again? You know it's against all rules.

PERCY: Me mates got liquor—
THOMAS: I don't want to know. [*To the* DURHAMS] Patient 12 could die any day. He should have died in Belgium. He should have died in England or on the journey here. I don't know why he hasn't.
VICTORIA: James had a great constitution. He is very strong. That's why he is alive and that's why he will get better.
THOMAS: How many times do…

He realises further argument with her is useless.

I don't wish to interfere with your visiting time. I know it's precious.

He turns to his desk. The DURHAMS *pass through the curtain.* THOMAS *stares at the inebriated* PERCY *who has managed to slide onto the desk.*

Oh, Percy, dear young Percy Groves. I first saw men like you in South Africa. They'd pray to God in the morning as the parson exhorted them to kill the men across the veldt who were at the same time praying to the same god. Poor old God, Percy. Fancy having to accommodate all those prayers from so many of the faithful. Better not to exist.

And I know, Percy, that your next question is: 'But, doc, how could you let this happen? The intelligent, educated, dedicated man that you are'.

He places an arm around PERCY *who grins at him.*

And I would say… that as an educated man I had the upmost faith in my superiors. They surely knew better than I. But two decades on, you, Percy, you are my answer to them. You are everything that I should have realised. You were the future.

PERCY *has nodded off on* THOMAS*'chest.*

Percy! [*Pause.*] No matter. It's all fine. Sleep, man, sleep.

THOMAS *lifts* PERCY *into his arms and exits. Lights down.*

Lights up. The DURHAMS *are seated outside the curtain. They remain there for some time, not speaking. Almost a vigil.*

DENMANN *emerges through the curtain. He nods and makes to exit, then stops and walks slowly over to the couple.*

DENMANN: Suppose I should say somethin'. I've seen you round here before. Could be your boy too?

VICTORIA: It is our—
> DURHAM *talks over his wife.*

DURHAM: That's right. The name's Durham. Alexander—and my wife Victoria.

DENMANN: Ed Denmann.

> *The men nod but do not shake hands.* VICTORIA *stares at the rough man. Silence.*

DURHAM: Um, it's a very trying show. Funny how a few letters on a man's skin can bring us together.

DENMANN: That's one way of lookin' at it.

DURHAM: Your lad's name?

DENMANN: Name was Andy. He was in the 5th.

DURHAM: Our James was in the 6th.

DENMANN: 5th, 6th, 99th. What does it matter? They all ended up dyin' for nothin'.

DURHAM: No, sir, no. That is not so.

VICTORIA: How dare you! How dare you! To say such a thing. 'They died for nothing'?

DENMANN: It's the truth, missus.

VICTORIA: It's a lie. A filthy lie.

DURHAM: It's alright.

DENMANN: I didn't come to get in a fight but I'm not gunna back away from what I believe to make you feel better. The war was pushed on us by the corrupt leaders of corrupt empires.

VICTORIA: My son, James, went to fight because it was the right thing to do. He lies there a hero.

DURHAM: He was fighting for Australia, sir, and the Empire.

DENMANN: He was fighting for the capitalists who didn't fight. And their sons who didn't fight. They made the guns and they sold the food. And got fat on it.

VICTORIA: Rubbish. We had to fight the Germans. It was life or death. Are you so ignorant that you know nothing of the rape of Belgian and French nuns? Of nurse Cavell? Of babies impaled on bayonets?

DENMANN: The same dirty propaganda that the Germans were told about Australian soldiers. Meant prisoners were hardly taken.

DURHAM: Our troops fought with honour.

DENMANN: Wars aren't fought with honour but with iron and steel and the flesh of young men. You're foolin' yourself to think other.

VICTORIA: This was a good war, a just war. It had to be fought and won. I will not abide being told by a man like you that my boy fought in vain.

DURHAM: We are proud of our boys and proud of our nation even if you are not.

DENMANN: I don't give a cuss about our nation. Don't care about any borders. I care about the people, decent working people of any type, any colour—

VICTORIA: Traitor!

DENMANN: I've been called that for five years. A badge of honour, missus.

DURHAM: Perhaps you should go.

DENMANN: Perhaps, my arse. I came to pay my respects to that body in the bed, as I did last week and the week before. I got as much right as anyone.

VICTORIA: He's not your son. He is James Durham.

DURHAM: Please, Victoria, you know what Dr Thomas says.

VICTORIA: Shut up! That is James. [*Rounding on* DENMANN] Your son is missing in action—good. By his death he covered himself in glory and so wouldn't have to face the shame of having you as a father.

DURHAM: No, Vic—

DENMANN: You got a lotta poison in you, missus. I might be a drunk and a brawler from the coal mines, but when it comes to pure bloody violence, I got nothin' on you.

    THOMAS *enters. The others don't see him.*

And you, mate. That's how you feel? I mean, you've lost a son too, despite what she says. You know that. You seem like a decent enough cove to me. So tell me this, does the death of, what is it now, 50,000, 60,000 men, mean that everythin's better? Does the doin' away with our young men like that make us better?

DURHAM: It shows a willingness of the nation to do the right thing, whatever the cost. [*Pause.*] There's been enough killing, too much. I understand what you say, sir, but I know in my heart that they have not died in vain. Victoria?

    The men look to VICTORIA *but she retains her icy resolve, turning away.*

THOMAS: Thank you, thank you for coming, yet again. Patient 12 remains … in a constant state of, well, suspension. You know I can't give you better news…

Look, I don't think it does any of us much good to dwell on the divisions caused by the war. Best to leave our politics at the door rather than bring discord into this place.

VICTORIA: I deserve a time and a place to reflect on my son and he [DENMANN] deprives me of that by his presence.

DENMANN: Rubbish!

THOMAS: You have the common ground of great loss. Can't you reflect on that?

DURHAM: In normal circumstances it would be a good idea, doctor. But these are not normal days. Too much has happened and all of it is bad. We are told, however, that time heals all wounds. Let us hope so.

VICTORIA: We won the war, Alexander! I find nothing bad about that when I think of the possibility of losing it. We have our freedoms. We have the Empire. In years to come, Australians, despite the best efforts of people like this [DENMANN], will come to celebrate the exploits of those who had the courage and the conviction to fight the Turks and the Germans.

I am now going to sit at the bed of one such hero.

VICTORIA *exits through the curtain.*

DURHAM *makes to exit, but stops.*

DURHAM: My son, wherever he lies, was a school cadet. At university he was for a time in the regiment there. He could have enlisted as an officer. He didn't. He saw himself as an ordinary citizen doing his duty. No airs, no graces. He was egalitarian. I think you should know that, Mr Denmann. [*Pause.*] Might you inform my wife that I'll be waiting for her in our automobile?

DURHAM *exits.*

THOMAS: Mrs Durham is… of strong material.
DENMANN: That she is.

Pause.

THOMAS: Never met a Wobbly before.
DENMANN: Haven't got two heads.

THOMAS: No, you look human. Thought most of you were doing hard labour in His Majesty's prisons?
DENMANN: That's up in Sydney. Some are doin' fifteen years for what Hughes calls sedition. Down here we get fined instead of jail but since we have no money we end up doin' a few weeks. And the wallopers don't go the bash here as much as Sydney. These blokes are long sufferin' workingmen so we got a bit in common. They're strugglin' against the set-up as much as anybody.
THOMAS: I'm afraid politics doesn't interest me, Mr Denmann.
DENMANN: I don't see how a man can shy away from it, doc. This country's headin' for an almighty stoush. You'll have to line up somewhere. You seen what's happened in Russia. That's the future.
THOMAS: I trust I don't have to line up against a wall at dawn. One hears stories about Russia.
DENMANN: Pure propaganda from the bosses' press. It's gunna be a whole new world—a workers' paradise—and Australia'll be in the vanguard because after there's no more cheering crowds, the soldiers'll find they're in the same lousy place they were before the war. They'll see reason and demand change. Just like in Munich right now—a workers' state.
THOMAS: The Returned Sailors and Servicemen's League reps who come here paint a very different picture. They talk of violent revolution.
DENMANN: That's the conservative union, the Billy Hughes union. Get any reps from the Soldiers Democratic League?
THOMAS: No.
DENMANN: That's because they're not allowed. Hughes and his cronies passed some regulations or some such.
THOMAS: That may well be so. I don't really know. I lost any political interest in the South African War. [*Pause.*] I lost a lot of things in that war. And like you, sir, I saw the future. Not quite your rosy, glorious prospect in Russia or Munich. I saw what precision artillery could do to men. And automatic gunfire while sodden generals still favoured the cavalry charge. And the wanton deaths of women and children.

    I'd like to say I took this job because I was some great… humanitarian. Working away in what is fast becoming a depository for battered bodies and lost souls. The fact is, it's the only job I can get. Something to do with discipline, or the lack of it.

Pause.

DENMANN: I follow you, doc. It's alright. [*Pause.*] I'm headin' off now. Reckon Mrs Durham was right about one thing. It's not my son over there.

THOMAS: Oh?

DENMANN: Na. He's too quiet. My lad would still be havin' a go at me even with his brains turned to mush. Truth is, doc, I don't really know. Just a hunch. I know you thought you was doin' the right thing, but I probably could have done without all this.

He offers THOMAS *his hand.*

Thanks anyway. Dunno if I'll be comin' back. Have to think on that.

THOMAS *accepts the handshake.*

THOMAS: I understand. We do what we can in the circumstances. I'll walk you out, Mr Denmann.

They exit.

Light change. PERCY *appears and goes to the curtain.*

PERCY: Leo. It's me. It's Percy. Come out.

LEO *emerges from the curtain.*

LEO: Not much time left, my friend.

PERCY: Weather's clear. Menin Road tomorrow or the day after. That's what they say.

LEO: That's right.

PERCY: Oh, Leo, it's been terrible, the last few weeks. I've been shooting horses. The shells don't kill them. Not all of them. They just lay there. Legs kicking out. Like their eyes were on fire. And no-one does anything. Shocking, shocking. I take care of them. Look after them. Make sure they suffer no more. They didn't ask to fight, Leo.

LEO: You're a good man, Percival Groves… lovely man.

LEO *embraces* PERCY *and moves off.*

PERCY: Don't go. Don't go.

LEO: For King and Country. That's what they reckon, ay Perce?

A final shared moment. LEO *exits to the bed.*

PERCY: No!

Light change. THOMAS *enters.*

THOMAS: Alright, Percy? It's late. You don't look too flash.

PERCY: Bit queer. Feel a… bit funny, doc.

THOMAS: You should be elsewhere. Haven't had any of that local fire water, have you?

PERCY: Maybe a little… Hard to get sometimes.

THOMAS *goes to the desk and takes a whiskey bottle and glasses from a drawer. He pours and sits on the desk.*

THOMAS: Join me for a drink, Percy?

PERCY: No allowed. Against the rules.

THOMAS: And who is the ranking medical official here tonight?

PERCY: You are, doc.

THOMAS: Exactly.

PERCY *makes his way to the desk.* THOMAS *pours.*

To us.

PERCY: Bottoms up… [*Indicating the bottle*] Why?

THOMAS: Well, sometimes I need a drink and sometimes I need company when I drink. [*Pause.*] And sometimes the rules that govern us don't matter anymore.

Lights partly down. Music—'Hello, Hello, Who's Your Lady Friend?'

Spotlight on ALICE. THOMAS *and* PERCY *drinking. The music slowly fades during her recital.*

ALICE: Dated 20/12/1919. Doctor. Please don't think bad of me for not coming to the funeral of the man who might have been Freddy Damiani. I don't think it was him. I really don't. Freddy seemed a bigger man than the one in the bed. Freddy was pretty solid. Also, if Freddy ever got a tattoo he wouldn't get one so small. Freddy would have the biggest and brightest tatt in his battalion. That was his nature. Another thing, Freddy didn't have any family I knew of, so why would he bother to put his name on his chest? Just makes no sense to me. No, it was definitely not Freddy.

We were going to get married as soon as he came home so his death—his death at Menin Road, not in the hospital—is a terrible thing for me to bear. We were a very close couple who would have had a very happy life together. I also feel very sorry for the other people who came in to look at the man. It was hard for them and I suppose his death is for the best, even if they don't think it at the moment.

Thank you, doctor.

Alice Bates.

The spotlight lingers on ALICE. *Fades.*

Lights up on THOMAS *and* PERCY, *still drinking.*

THOMAS: A toast. A toast to the young Major Charles Thomas off to the veldt, to the Transvaal, full of Imperial pomp.

PERCY: To… to pompous Thomas.

THOMAS: Very good. Spot on, Percy

PERCY *is very pleased with himself.*

Lights are low on the pair. Spotlight on DURHAM.

DURHAM: Dated 20/12/1919. Dear Dr Thomas. A note to thank you for your diligence regarding this young warrior. Even though his death was not unexpected, it was still a shock to Victoria and to me. The Department of Defence service was well conducted at Cheltenham and we both drew great comfort from the words of the clergy. The Biblical quotations were most apt and as they were spoken by both Protestant and Catholic ministers I have hope that all Australians will put aside their differences and work together in what certainly will be difficult years. One small note of optimism amid the sorrow.

Yours.

Alexander Durham.

Spotlight down. THOMAS *and* PERCY *at the desk in semi-light.*

THOMAS: A toast, a toast to the humble Dr Charles Thomas, off to the dormitories and wards of the Caulfield Military Hospital, wallowing in his own despair and disappointment.

PERCY: To the… the disappointing doc.

Lights low on the duo. Spotlight up on DENMANN.

DENMANN: Dated 22/12/1919. To Dr Thomas. Thanks for what it is that you have done. I don't want to think on the death too much. If it was Andy then he was a goner long before they bothered to ship him home. You said he was as good as dead and I took you at your word. A funeral with priests and prayers was not what he would have wanted. Very much not what I wanted. There's a lot of horseshit going about. Seems every town is putting up some sort of memorial to honour their dead boys. Best if they had kept them at home alive. Andy was a good lad. Better than me.

Edward Denmann.

Spotlight down.

Lights up on THOMAS *and* PERCY, *quite drunk.* THOMAS *intent on talking,* PERCY *intent on drinking.*

THOMAS: Twenty years ago, Percy. Twenty years? God, I am getting bloody old. Anyway, off I went to Africa, off for a short, sharp war. None of us took any notice that this happened to be the second short, sharp war against the Boers. No, this was different. [*Pause.*] Witness… witnessing science and warfare combining. All the elements waiting to take the stage of Turkey and France and wherever else the wretched thing could find a roost. That right, Percy?

PERCY: … Right, doc.

THOMAS: You're a good man to talk to, Percy.

PERCY *nods.*

Spotlight on VICTORIA. THOMAS *and* PERCY *again in low light.*

VICTORIA: Dated 12/1/1920. Dear Dr Thomas. May I offer my heartfelt appreciation for your work on behalf of James? I believe that my husband has already expressed his thanks but I wish to plainly state that I was grateful for the precious time I had with my son before his death. He was my gift to the nation and I gave of him freely. This will be a greater nation because of his sacrifice. And that of so many young men of his calibre. Their blood sacrifice will make us great.

Regards.

Victoria Durham.

Spotlight down. Lights up on THOMAS *and* PERCY, *drunk.*

PERCY: [*singing very badly*] You, you… can see them sigh… you can see them die—

THOMAS: And a very bad man to listen to. No more, please.

PERCY: Sorry, doc. It was Leo's favourite.

THOMAS *looks across to the curtain. It parts a little. The doctor reacts.*

THOMAS: Come on, Percy. Time to get you back to your dormitory.

PERCY: No more fire water?

THOMAS: Let's save a little for later.

He gently escorts PERCY *out.* THOMAS *stands, looking to the curtain.*

Light change. Music up—'It's a Long Way to Tipperary'.

PATIENT 12 *appears through the curtain, again the AIF soldier.* THOMAS *is no longer drunk.*

PATIENT 12: Time, sir?

THOMAS: I think so.

PATIENT 12: Righto then.

A formal nod. PATIENT 12 *walks to centre stage.*

Light change. The kith and kin now join him for a traditional portrait prior to embarkation. Quite formal. This is basically a light flash with the 'phoomp' camera sound. First DURHAM *and* VICTORIA, *then* ALICE, *then* DENMANN *(surly), finally* PERCY.

They exit the space. The music fades.

PATIENT 12 *remains.* THOMAS *still near the curtain, waiting.*

THOMAS: All done?

PATIENT 12 *nods, moves to* THOMAS *and without ado they go through the curtain. Music—the complete second verse of 'Roses of Picardy'.*

Lights down to dark followed by backlighting of THOMAS *removing the tubes from* PATIENT 12. *He then takes the pillow from under the boy's head and gently smothers him. He replaces the tubes. Lights to black for an extended time. The music fades.*

Lights up on THOMAS *at his desk. The curtain no longer covers the empty bed.* PERCY *enters with a rough kit. He has removed the blue armband.*

Don't tell me, Percy—you're leaving us.

PERCY: … That's right, doc.

THOMAS: You realise that you can't do that? Papers need signing, you understand.
PERCY: Know that. You told me that.
THOMAS: And yet you're going?
PERCY: That's… right.
THOMAS: I could call for orderlies to come and tie you to your bed. You know that?
Pause. Then they smile.
Where might you be going?
PERCY: Not sure. Can't stay here though. All mad here.
THOMAS: Very true. We are, all of us, stark staring mad. Me most of all, I think.
PERCY: No, not you. Not you. You're a good man… Leo liked you. Liked you a lot. He told me. He said you were going to help him, to make him die. To put him… to rest. I got mad but he said it was… all for the best.
Pause.
THOMAS: Did he, Percy?
PERCY: And he told me not to be afraid. Not to have dreams… no thoughts, no thoughts.
THOMAS: Percy, before you go—listen to me. You've suffered nerve damage. I imagine you've been told all that.
PERCY: Don't know what… what I've been told.
THOMAS: It's not my area, Percy, but what happened to you, the constant bombardment, has affected your mind. That is your condition—shell shock. That's what you have. It's now commonly recognised and advances are being—
PERCY: Leo told me to tell you… that it wasn't. He told me to tell you—because he said you were decent, decent but grumpy—that it was… other stuff.
THOMAS: Yes?
PERCY: Rifleman—that was me. Very good. But never took dead aim… always shot up, follow? Never saw a man fall from my gun. Never looked.
THOMAS: I can understand. I gather a lot of men—
PERCY: No! No, listen! Nothing to do with bombs and rifles. From

nowhere, at night, Germans in my trench. Or I'm in theirs. Who knows? Bayonets, clubs, shouting... All our blood was up. 'No prisoners!' Fritz and me together. We looked at each other. Then, 'Kamarade', he cries and smiles at me. His hands are up. Could have grabbed him, could have pushed him behind the line. Didn't. I pushed my bayonet into his throat. Here. [*He indicates the space between the collarbon*es.] Keep pushing, pushing... till he stops screaming and flapping.

Long pause.

Could not get my steel out of him. Went too low. Got stuck in his bones... Pushed and pulled him about. Left him there with my bayonet and his white eyes and smiley teeth. Like all the poor dead horses.

THOMAS: Percy, listen. There's a new department devoted to repatriation. Hopefully it will control all facets of care and attention. That means you'll be taken care of. You will have somewhere to go and be treated, rather than sitting in a corner making baskets. No need to go.

PERCY: Leo told me it was for the best... like him dying. Best for me on the road. In the bush. Good there.

THOMAS: Alright, Percy. Go where you must.

PERCY: Go back to the Kiewa... Very nice. Mum got sick of me last time, but this time... She thought I was mad. I don't care. Can't stay here. Mad here making baskets... I'll keep walking in the bush.

THOMAS: Then the best of luck.

PERCY: Luck? All used up over there, eh, doc?... Don't you reckon? No luck for anyone, anymore? Eh? [*Pause.*] I'm just a... bit buggered, doc. What's in my head. Stays there. Can't get it out.

PERCY *takes his kit and starts to exit.*

THOMAS: Sorry about your friend.

PERCY *stops and turns.*

PERCY: Leo was my life. Leo was all of me. You... took him, doc, but... the best result—for the others.

As he exits, music up—'Pack Up Your Troubles in Your Old Kit Bag'.

THOMAS *is at his desk. Lights slowly fade. The music fades.*

THE END

presents
PATIENT 12
23 April–11 May 2014

Writer
Kevin Summers

Director
Don Mackay

Designer
Sophie Woodward

Lighting Designer
Bronwyn Pringle

Stage Manager
Chris Martin

Assistant Stage Manager
Libby Wilhelm

Dr Charles Thomas: **Jason Buckley**
Alexander Durham: **Colin MacPherson**
Victoria Durham: **Jenny Seedsman**
Percy Groves: **Joel Parnis**
Edward Denmann: **Dennis Coard**
Alice Bates: **Heidi Valkenberg**
Patient 12, James Durham, Andy Denmann, Freddie Damiani and Leo:
Will Ewing

Production supported by The Cybec Foundation

LA MAMA

Level 1, 205 Faraday Street, Carlton VIC 3053
www.lamama.com.au info@lamama.com.au
facebook.com/lamama.theatre twitter.com/lamamatheatre
Office phone 03 9347 6948 Office Hours Mon–Fri, 10:30am–5:30pm

CEO & Artistic Director
Liz Jones

Company Manager
Caitlin Dullard

Marketing Coordinator
Mary Helen Sassman

Communications Coordinator
Nedd Jones

House Managers
Rebecca Etchell & Amber Hart

La Mama Learning Producer
Maureen Hartley

Preservation Coordinator
Fiona Wiseman

La Mama for Kids Curator
Ella Holmes

La Mama Musica Curator
Annabel Warmington

La Mama Poetica Curator
Amanda Anastasi

Script Appraiser
Graham Downey

FRONT OF HOUSE STAFF:
The regular staff and Jo-Anne Armstrong, Susan Bamford-Caleo, Alex Desebrock, Carmelina Di Guglielmo, Nicola Gunn, Tanya Harrowell, Amber Hart, Mari Lourey, Phil Roberts, Laurence Strangio, Annabel Warmington, Rebecca Mezei and Robyn Clancy.

COMMITTEE OF MANAGEMENT:
Sue Broadway, Caroline Lee, Dur-é Dara, Mark Rubbo, Kerry Noonan, Adam Cass, Richard Watts and Liz Jones.

La Mama Theatre is on traditional Wurundjeri land, part of the Kulin nation, and the Committee of Management, Staff and wider theatrical community acknowledge its traditional custodians.

La Mama is financially assisted by the Australian Government through the Australia Council – its Arts Funding and advisory body, the Victorian Government through Arts Victoria – Department of Premier and Cabinet, and the City of Melbourne through the Arts and Culture Triennial Funding program. Our thanks to the management and staff at Readings Bookshop, for their continued support.

KEVIN SUMMERS
PLAYWRIGHT

Kevin Summers has tertiary qualifications in law, arts and education, and has worked as a performer, playwright, teacher and director. His plays include *The Empty Say*, *Salvation Jane* and *Blamey*. Much seen on television, he has been a core cast member of *Cop Shop*, *Prisoner*, *Neighbours* and the much acclaimed *Phoenix*, and had continuing guest roles in scores of shows and mini-series. Most recently on stage in the Australian premiere season of Neil La Bute's monologue, *Wrecks*.

DON MACKAY
DIRECTOR

Shows **Don Mackay** has staged include *Wild World* the Cat Stevens Story, *The Carer* with Bud Tingwell and *Under Milk Wood* with Michael Craig (for McPherson Touring), *The Book Club* with Amanda Muggleton (for International Concert Attractions), *Sleuth*, *Stevie*, *Same Time Next Year*, *Chapter Two* and *Flexitime*. He has also directed productions for Adelaide Festival Centre, Perth Festival, Arts Centre Melbourne, Hothouse Theatre, Knockabout Theatre, La Mama, Ensemble and the Melbourne Theatre Company. Don has made a number of adaptations for the stage including *Puckoon* by Spike Milligan, *Act One* by Moss Hart and recreations of the classic radio era—*Lux Radio Theatre* and *Tune in Tomorrow*.

SOPHIE WOODWARD
DESIGNER

After graduating from the Victorian College of the Arts, **Sophie Woodward** has made a distinct contribution to a diverse range of productions. This has included: set and costume design for *The Pyjama Girl*, directed by Travis Dowling at HotHouse Theatre; set and costume design for *4000 miles*, directed by Mark Pritchard and set design for *Day One: A Hotel, Evening*, directed by Gary Abrahams at Red Stitch Theatre; set design for *The Long Days Dying*, directed by Kevin Summers and *Conspiracy*, directed by Peta Coy at La Mama Courthouse; and, costume design for *Document*, choreographed by Sandra Parker at Dancehouse.

BRONWYN PRINGLE
LIGHTING DESIGN

Bronwyn Pringle is a Melbourne based lighting designer whose work with companies including Polyglot, SoulArt and Chamber Made Opera has been seen in venues ranging from a derelict Kensington flat, Belvoir St, a warehouse in Buenos Aries, the Segerstrom Centre in California and many more. She has won Green Room Awards for *Letters from Animals* (SRWT/Here Theatre) and *Alias Grace* (Malthouse, originally presented at La Mama) and two Melbourne Fringe Festival Design Awards. Other design highlights include *My Life in the Nude*, *Aviary*, *Two Mortals*, *Serial Blogger*, *The Hatpin*, *A Kind of Fabulous Hatred*, *The Flood* and *Lloyd Beckmann: Beekeeper*.

CHRIS MARTIN
STAGE MANAGER

Chris 'Chuck' Martin has been a hospitality stalwart for close to 14 years. In 2013 he completed a Diploma of Live Production in Theatre, Lighting and Sound at Box Hill TAFE to complement his abilities to hang out in dark, noisy places with interesting people. 2013 was also a good year for working in theatre where he worked on *Sweeney Todd*, *The Woodsmen* and *39 Steps*.

JASON BUCKLEY
ACTOR

Jason Buckley is a graduate, B.A Drama & Media, Deakin University (Rusden) and Post Grad Dip Ed Drama & Media, Melbourne University. His previous La Mama Courthouse appearances include: *Bon Lives* (1995), *Sin Bin* (2001), *Mouth of The Dog* (2003) and *Melborn* (2008). *Silencia* (2004) and *Dimboola* (2008), are amongst his favourite previous La Mama productions. Jason acted with Kevin Summers in *Silencia* and reunites in *Patient 12*, with Kevin as writer, 10 years later. Recent TV credits include: *Betterman*, *Mrs Biggs*, *Media Giants – Magazine Wars*, *Utopia*, *Wentworth and Films*, *John Doe* and *Dream Children* By day Jason works in the Staging Department at GTV 9.

DENNIS COARD
ACTOR

Dennis Coard is an Irish-born actor and writer, and a graduate of the VCA. Theatre work includes Don Mackay's *Act One* and a dozen plays with MTC. Television work includes guest roles on most TV dramas and six years in the leading role of 'Michael' on *Home and Away*. Main film work includes *Amy*, *Noise*, *The Jammed* and the leading role in the AFI winning *Return Home*. Recent work includes *It's A Date*, *Dr. Blake Mysteries*, *The Broken Shore* and the role of Billy Hughes in *Monash & The Forgotten Anzac*. Dennis regularly performs his own one-man show *The Fall of the Roman Umpire*. He is a proud ambassador for Barnardos Australia—the Children's Charity.

WILL EWING
ACTOR

Will Ewing is a Melbourne-based actor, director, writer, musician and voice over artist. The youngest of ten children, Will moved to Melbourne from his family farm in southwest Victoria to study an Advanced Diploma of Acting at the National Theatre Drama School. It was there that he became the recipient of the sought after Basin Theatre scholarship and G&E scholarship two years in a row. Since graduating, Will has worked tirelessly both on stage and screen. On television, Will has played the loveable rogue on *Neighbours* (2011–2012), appeared on *Miss Fisher's Murder Mysteries* (2013), and recently played the role of the Time Traveller in the latest promotional campaign for RACQ (2013–2014). After appearing in the short films *Box Head* (2012), Sway (2012), *Splendour* (2013) and *Still Water* (2013), Will both featured in and directed the popular short film *Speed Date* (2013). He has also made his mark on the Melbourne theatre scene with starring roles in *The McNeil Project* (2012), and *Cruising Paradise* (2013) and *A Chekov Triptych* (2013).

COLIN MACPHERSON
ACTOR

JOEL PARNIS
ACTOR

Colin MacPherson has worked extensively for the past thirty years as an actor and director in Canada and Australia. As an actor he continues to be heavily involved in the Melbourne Theatre community, having worked with La Mama in *Porcelain*, Viscious Fish Theatre, Human Sacrifice Theatre in *Glengarry Glen Ross, Speed The Plow, One Flew Over The Cuckoos Nest*, Larrikin Productions' *The Reindeer Monologues*, to name a few. Memorable productions over the years include *The Dresser, Sleuth, Hamlet* and *Amadeus*. Recently Colin has been in TV series including *City Homicide, The Hollowmen, The Saddle Club, Neighbours* and *M.D.A.* Feature films include *Parallels, Blonde (The Marilyn Monroe story), John Doe* and as Lester in *The Caretaker*. Other films include *The Trial Of Film, Mului* and *Samaritan*. Colin also wrote and produced the documentary *Shore Stories (Tales Of A Kiosk)*, as well as the upcoming short film *Disappearance Of A Politician*. Colin is very pleased to be a part of this inaugural production of *Patient 12*.

Joel Parnis has a BA (Music Theatre) from Ballarat Arts Academy. With a great passion for history, Joel is extremely excited to work with Don and the cast of *Patient 12* in his first La Mama show. Music Theatre: *Les Miserables* Cameron Mackintosh's 25th Anniversary Tour (Opening July 2014); *The Producers* (Lead Tenor), *Chess, The Pirates of Penzance* for The Production Company; *Flowerchildren: the Mamas and Papas Story* (Papa Denny U/S), *Godspell* for Magnormos; *Atlantis in Concert*. Regional Tours: *Tune in Tomorrow*, directed by Don Mackay; *Cinderella*. Other Credits: Universal Studios Singapore (Singer/Dancer); original member of *Golden Oldies* cabaret group, touring nationally.

JENNY SEEDSMAN
ACTOR

Jenny Seedsman's many stage credits include stints with the QTC, TN and MTC and, of course, Don Mackay's *Lux Radio Theatre*. She has also narrated over a hundred audio books over the years, including T*he Getting of Wisdom* for The ABC Heritage Series. TV credits include *Blue Heelers*, *Neighbours*, *Stingers*, *Twentysomething*, *The Dr. Blake Mysteries* and so many others that she has forgotten half of them! She is currently also touring regularly in Alan Hopgood's Health Plays and has recently ventured into the world of Theatre Restaurant with appearances at Taggart's Restaurant in Frankston.

HEIDI VALKENBURG
ACTOR

Displaying a strong interest in the performing arts at a young age, at age ten Heidi was cast in ABC's children's series *Book Bugs*. Falling deeply in love with the art of acting, Heidi has been working in the film and television industry steadily since. Some of her screen credits include *Blue Heelers*, *CrashZone2*, *Something In The Air*, *Neighbours*, *Tangle2*, *KidsWB* (co host), *Winners and Losers*, and *Underbelly*. She has also appeared in the recent miniseries *Jack Irish*, the feature *I love you too*, ABC's highly acclaimed comedy series *It's A Date* as well as the newly released independent feature *Bound by Blue*. Recent stage credits include the Melbourne International Comedy Festival's production of *The Gift* (Anthony Noak) *Oh the humanity! And other good intentions* (Act-O-matic3000) and *No names no pack dri*l (Pine Heights Theatre). Heidi has studied internationally as well as on home soil and when not traipsing the boards or appearing in front of the camera is also a visual artist and has exhibited her painted photography works with great success.

STANDING OVATION FOR
AUSTRALIA'S HOME OF INDEPENDENT THEATRE

In 2014, La Mama will celebrate 47 years of nurturing new Australian theatre.

Built in 1883 for Anthony Reuben Ford, a Carlton printer, the building at 205 Faraday Street had been used as a workshop, a boot and shoe factory, an electrical engineering workshop and a silk underwear factory before becoming a theatre in 1967. La Mama was established by Betty Burstall and modelled on experimental theatre activities at La MaMa E.T.C., New York. Jack Hibberd's play *Three Old Friends* was the first play performed in the tiny space.

Since that time the crowded intimacy of La Mama has provided welcome opportunities to a host of playwrights, actors, directors, technicians, film-makers, poets and comedians, such as David Williamson, Barry Dickins, John Romeril, Tes Lyssiotis, Lloyd Jones, Arthur and Corinne Cantrill, Judith Lucy, Richard Frankland, Julia Zemiro, and Cate Blanchett... the list of those who have been nurtured there is long.

Under the capable care of Liz Jones (Artistic Director since 1976), and her La Mama team, more than 50 productions are now produced annually at La Mama, and at our second performance venue, the refurbished La Mama Courthouse, 349 Drummond Street. An ever-increasing audience is drawn not only from the Carlton and Melbourne University environs, but from far and wide across the country.

'I set La Mama up, as a space for writers and directors to perform in but also it was a space where people came, as audience, to participate in the creative experiment.'
—Betty Burstall, 1987, Artistic Director of La Mama 1967–76

'Much will be said of La Mama's role in developing a new generation of Australian writing. However, in considering policies and personalities, one should not forget the nature of the space and its impact in making possible performances that would be lost in a large theatre. It gave performances the intimacy of the cinema close-up with the exciting immediacy of the live theatre and the warmth of the coffee lounge.'
—Daryl Wilkinson, 1986, Director
From *La Mama... The story of a Theatre*

La Mama Theatre—which, on various occasions, has been called headquarters, the source, the shopfront and the birthplace of Australian theatre—was classified by the National Trust in 1999.

'The two story brick building is of State cultural significance because it has been occupied by La Mama Theatre... The building is indelibly associated with the performance arts and is a rare manifestation of an experimental theatre in Australia...'
—National Trust Classification Report

When it comes to grassroots Melbourne theatre, La Mama in Carlton is like the 60GB iPod—small, subtle, but containing a whole lot more than you might expect.
—John Bailey, *The Age*. E.G. 29/06/05

La Mama produces work from two venues: 205 Faraday Street, Carlton (opposite top), and at the La Mama Courthouse, 349 Drummond Street, Carlton.

For current La Mama productions and events, see www.lamama.com.au

www.ingramcontent.com/pod-product-compliance
Lightning Source LLC
Chambersburg PA
CBHW050027090426
42734CB00021B/3451